# Canadian Georgian Furniture

## Donald Blake Webster

The cost of this book
has been subsidized
by the
**RUTH HOME
MEMORIAL FUND**
established by the
members of the
Museums Section of
The Ontario Historical Society

**RŌM**
Royal Ontario Museum

© Royal Ontario Museum, 1981
100 Queen's Park, Toronto, Ontario, Canada M5S 2C6
ISBN 0-88854-262-3
Printed and bound in Canada by THE ALGER PRESS

**Canadian Cataloguing in Publication Data**
   Webster, Donald Blake, 1933–
      Canadian Georgian furniture
   (ROM insight series)
   ISBN 0-88854-262-3

1. Furniture, Georgian—Canada—History.
2. Furniture—Canada—History.   I. Royal Ontario
Museum.   II. Title.   III. Series.

NK2441.W42      749.211      C81-094182-1

Front cover: Sofa table, Ontario, Napanee
area, c. 1810-20 (see page 18).

# Canadian Georgian Furniture

The earliest furniture produced in Canada was, of course, made in Quebec, the first area to be settled, and in wholly French styles. A small quantity of this furniture has even survived from the 17th century.

In the 17th and early 18th centuries, all of southeastern Canada was included in the colony of New France, and French influence reached west to the Prairies and south to the Great Lakes watershed and the Mississippi Valley. English colonies in America at that time extended only from the Atlantic Ocean to the Appalachian Mountains. After 1670, England's sole presence in Canada was the Hudson's Bay Company in the North.

The half-century after the fall of New France in 1760 brought great changes in the size and composition of the population of Canada. These led to a rapid expansion of settlement of the huge land mass—far beyond anything the small French population had ever attempted. The American Revolution, events in Scotland, and wars in Europe created large displaced populations. From the 1780s on, Canada became home for many of these people, particularly for American Loyalist and Scottish refugees.

Although English-speaking settlers, largely from the New England colonies, had migrated to coastal Nova Scotia and New Brunswick as early as the 1740s, the conditions and economies of their first settlements were far too primitive to attract craftsmen or to generate the production of what today we would call decorative arts. This remained true in rural and frontier areas even decades later. When the Reverend James MacGregor came to Pictou, Nova Scotia, in 1786, he found Scottish settlers who had arrived there in 1773 still living in log huts chinked with moss and roofed with bark. This is how he described their living conditions:

> Their furniture was of the rudest description. Frequently a block of wood or a rude bench, made out of a slab, in which four sticks had been inserted as legs, served for chair or table. Their food was commonly served up in wooden dishes or in wooden plates, and eaten with wooden spoons. Money was scarcely seen, and almost all trade was done by barter.

These were obviously not conditions conducive to the production of fine or elegant furniture, but only of homemade necessities.

The earliest known and recorded English cabinetmaker in Canada was Edward Draper, who arrived in 1749 with the Cornwallis expedition, which founded and settled Halifax. Draper is known to have made ladder-back chairs and may have fabricated other furniture as well. In 1780 Joseph DeGant established Canada's first furniture factory in Halifax where he made Windsor chairs, many of which, marked under the seats, still survive. Simple utilitarian chairs, however, were not fine furniture.

By the mid-1780s, populations had increased and towns had grown. Halifax, Saint John, Quebec, and Montreal were on the way to becoming sophisticated cities. The crafting of formal and elegant furniture, which depended on this sort of urban structure, began in British North America only in the mid-1780s, and coincided with the heavy influx of American Loyalists and Scots. Among them, superior craftsmen now also began to gravitate to Canada, with some reasonable expectation that they might be able to make a living from their specialized skills and training.

## Styles of the 18th Century

Towards the end of the 18th century, the prevailing style of English furniture was the late Chippendale form, named after Thomas Chippendale who had first published his design book *The Gentleman and Cabinet-maker's Director* in 1753. This style had gradually evolved in Britain during the 18th century, and in many variations was the standard of modern elegance throughout the English-speaking world by the 1780s and 1790s.

Many, and perhaps most, of the few first-generation English-speaking Canadians able to afford the trappings of elegance preferred English furnishings, which were easily transported by ship as settlers' goods or as imports. Still, there was plenty of business available for local cabinet-makers capable of producing finer furniture in English styles.

PREFERENCE FOR MAHOGANY

Just as in Britain and the United States, so in English Canada mahogany was the preferred wood for sophisticated furniture. Since it was not native to Canada, it had to be imported from the West Indies. Mahogany logs were carried as ballast cargo in sailing vessels and were landed at seaport cities from Halifax to Montreal. Because of their great weight, the logs could be transported only by water, for the few existing roads of that period were far too rough to tolerate heavy loads. Thus we have no evidence of the early use of mahogany or of the crafting of mahogany furniture in areas beyond very short distances from the seaport cities. Inland cabinetmakers used native substitutes such as cherry, birch, butternut, maple, and walnut.

In the 1780s and 1790s the number of cabinetmakers and other craftsmen increased throughout English Canada. They set up shops and small factories wherever markets for their wares existed, and the production of chairs and other articles of furniture began to flourish. Nonetheless, homemade and carpenter-made furniture of pine and simple factory-made articles on the order of ladderback and Windsor chairs were still the norm, and in frontier areas remained so for many decades. In urban areas, however, elegant mahogany furniture in various styles and degrees of sophistication began to appear between 1785 and 1790. Many of the finest examples of formal English-Canadian furniture that still exist were, in fact, made before about 1810.

Although most of the cabinetmakers known from before 1825 operated in Nova Scotia and New Brunswick, many others established themselves in Quebec and Montreal. From Montreal, particularly, came some of the finest Canadian Georgian furniture known, though no early Montreal piece has yet been identified to a specific maker.

Upper Canada in this period was still the agricultural frontier. At present no cabinetmaker in Upper Canada is known by name from before about 1810. Nonetheless, excellent examples of turn-of-the-century maple and cherry furniture survive from the Kingston and eastern Lake Ontario region and from the Niagara Peninsula. There were skilled furniture makers in Upper Canada, probably before 1800, but because of the lack of early newspapers, advertising, and other records, we cannot yet trace specific people.

Many cabinetmakers and other craftsmen could not depend solely on their specialty for their livelihood. Most had to diversify into other related areas of activity. In slack times, cabinetmakers often accepted contracts for ship and house interiors. Some advertised not only as cabinetmakers but also as upholsterers, finishers, and painters, or as lumber and paint merchants. Most bought, restored, and sold used furniture. In the 19th century many also imported English furniture and sold it along with the furniture they themselves made. Always a mainstay for cabinetmakers was undertaking, for they built the coffins that were constantly in demand.

## Styles and Fashions of the 19th Century

English Canadians who could afford finer furniture were generally conservative in their tastes. Thus we find that their furniture was designed according to styles that were already current and accepted in England, with the result that cabinetmakers in Canada had little scope for design innovation.

The generic Chippendale forms of the late 18th century were succeeded by the Sheraton, Hepplewhite, and Regency styles of the late 18th and early 19th centuries, after they had become accepted in England. In early 19th-century Canadian furniture, these post-Chippendale forms were often mixed. Characteristics of two or three different design styles from published design books of the period were often combined in the same piece of furniture.

We must remember that at that period—before the advent of modern advertising and the promotion of producer-created styles—new fashions were largely initiated in English court circles. Fashions that had been accepted by the upper levels of English society, perhaps because they were pushed by a favoured Royal Appointment cabinetmaker, were imitated and adapted throughout the English-speaking world. Canadian cabinetmakers did not, of course, enjoy the status of official favour or Royal Appointment. Even if they had been capable of creating new design forms, they did not have sufficient influence on fashion to make them widely accepted.

## Scarcity of Surviving Furniture

The so-called Georgian styles in furniture—the Chippendale, succeeded by the Sheraton, Hepplewhite, and Regency—prevailed in Canada until about 1830. Unfortunately this furniture is rather scarce today, for only a little of what was produced has survived. The reason for this is not so much that it was deliberately discarded as that it perished in fires. In the 19th century, when buildings were heated by wood-burning fireplaces, houses, and all they contained, burnt down with great regularity. This, coupled with the fact that many cabinetmakers did not work at their craft full time, leaves us today with a relatively small body of surviving work from which to judge the real excellence of the furniture that was produced.

Many items of general-purpose furniture, such as chests of drawers and drop-leaf tables, survive in far greater numbers than do special-purpose pieces, such as clocks, card tables, and corner chairs. Obviously far fewer of the latter were made. Since most houses were heated by a central chimney and fireplace, which also served for cooking, the kitchen, simply furnished with chairs and a big all-purpose table, was the centre of all activity. Other rooms, including bedrooms, were unheated and minimally furnished. Obviously there was no call for special-purpose furniture in these houses in which the families essentially wintered in the kitchen—except to sleep.

Before about 1830, expensive clocks were restricted to the wealthy. Tall standing clocks, the most luxurious items of early English-Canadian furniture, were to be found in only a very small minority of households, and the same was true of tall four-poster beds and of upholstered sofas.

Special-occasion furniture, such as elegant dining tables and sets of chairs, serving sideboards, and wine cellarets, was useful only in large houses with multiple or end-wall fireplaces, and so was parlour furniture, such as card tables, sofas and sofa tables, upholstered chairs, and desks. Thus, since the proportion of houses that could be fully heated and occupied in winter was small, special-purpose furniture was always far less common than general-purpose furniture.

## Identification

Unlike the furniture of French Canada, the furniture of English Canada of the Georgian period is not readily identified by design and styles alone. It is, in fact, very similar to furniture that was being made in England, Scotland, and the northeastern United States during the same period. Thus the great problem in isolating the rather rare Canadian furniture is that of identification.

WOODS  Positive identification of wood is perhaps the single most important factor in identifying early Canadian furniture. The hardwoods used were imported mahogany and native birch, cherry, maple, walnut, and butternut. Generally they were combined with pine, and usually pine alone, as a secondary wood—the hidden wood of furniture used for underlying frames, drawer structures, or surfaces under veneers. Although secondary pine was very often used in American furniture as well, there it was commonly combined with other secondary woods. In English furniture, the secondary wood was frequently oak, which was almost never used in Canadian furniture.

In addition to a secondary wood of pine alone, early Canadian furniture often has a combination of exterior woods, which provides a good clue to where a piece may have been made. In Ontario, for example, a combination of striking bird's-eye maple or curly maple and cherry was extremely common. Ontario is also the only area where walnut was used, for it is the only province to which walnut is native.

In Quebec, while mahogany furniture was made in Montreal and Quebec, butternut and curly and bird's-eye maple were very common cabinet woods in the Eastern Townships south of the St. Lawrence. Butternut furniture is, in fact, common only in the geographical growth range of the tree, the Eastern Townships and the Saint John River valley in New Brunswick. In the Maritimes, particularly in Nova Scotia and New Brunswick, we find a very heavy use of birch, sometimes alone, but often combined with maple, and sometimes even with mahogany. Birch was a common cabinet wood in the northeastern United States as well, but it was not typically used elsewhere in Canada. Since the native woods of Eastern Canada and those of the northeastern United States are very often the same, the problem of identification arises not in distinguishing Canadian furniture from English, but in distinguishing Canadian furniture from American.

DETAILS OF
CRAFTSMANSHIP  In the identification process, there may be a basis for an obvious conclusion, perhaps solid historical information about a piece of furniture, or even a maker's marking on the piece itself. In many cases, however, we must look at the details of style and the techniques of craftsmanship. We do not, for example, find Canadian Georgian furniture with wholly veneered surfaces, or with extremely elaborate inlay work, since the

market for which this furniture was produced could not generally afford the cost of such opulence.

Most early English-Canadian furniture, though made of good woods and well designed and constructed, is rather austere and simple, without extreme ornamentation. In the same way, sometimes even the best of Canadian Georgian furniture incorporates obvious simplifications or shortcuts in construction. Bow-front chests of drawers, for example, are uncommon, and serpentine fronts are rare. Imported English hardware was expensive and often hard to come by, so that much of the early English-Canadian furniture has plain wooden knobs on drawers, even on pieces that obviously deserved something better.

We often find furniture constructed of mixed woods, with the best wood reserved for the face of the piece, be it a table, a chest of drawers, or a cupboard, and the less desirable wood used for sides and tops. Veneering, too, was typically applied only to certain parts of a piece of furniture, and often only to the front.

Still, the points of difference in detail between furniture made in Canada and that made in the northeastern United States are often minute and at best inexact. Thus in considering the characteristics of furniture produced by peoples whose cultural sameness was far stronger than their differences, we cannot arrive at absolute national or regional distinctions in the early furniture and other decorative arts produced in adjoining regions of the two countries.

Once whatever conclusions possible have been reached from wood identification and construction details, it becomes necessary to look at historical information. Most earlier Canadian furniture has been moved so often that it has been completely separated from any historical context. Sometimes, however, a piece is accompanied by historical evidence, or by someone's belief regarding its origin, generally dependent on word-of-mouth information, but occasionally documented in early letters or diaries.

Certainly the most solid evidence is a cabinetmaker's marking on the piece itself, but this unfortunately is very rare. Only two Canadian cabinetmakers working before 1825 are known to have put paper labels on their furniture: Thomas Nisbet of Saint John, New Brunswick, and Tulles, Pallister & McDonald of Halifax, Nova Scotia. Some fifty labelled

HISTORICAL
INFORMATION

Thomas Nisbet pieces are known to have survived, but only two known Tulles, Pallister & McDonald pieces exist. Other makers very occasionally marked their work in pencil. More than ninety-nine per cent of early 19th-century Canadian furniture, however, carries no markings or inherent evidence of its maker.

For historical information, certainly good documentation is the best and most reliable source, but that too is rare. Evidence for the origin of a piece of furniture most frequently comes in the form of passed-on family history, which is not always accurate. Often, in fact, a piece of furniture is backed by a family history that could not possibly correspond to the style and date of the piece itself. All word-of-mouth evidence must thus be treated with some suspicion.

All in all, finding and identifying Georgian-period Canadian furniture requires both careful observation and experience. Furniture does not break down neatly into categories, nor can it be identified as precisely as natural species of plants or animals, for furniture was created by human beings, with all their infinite capacity for variation.

The furniture of eastern Canada and that of the northeastern United States have the greatest similarity and thus are the most difficult to identify with certainty. In looking at pieces long removed from any known family or historical background, it may sometimes be plainly impossible to arrive at firm conclusions about whether they are of Canadian or of American origin. All one can do in such cases is to decide that a piece is the one or is the other beyond a reasonable doubt.

In probably the larger number of cases, however, one can reasonably base a conclusion that a piece of furniture is or is not Canadian on the mixture of woods in it, or on its last known location in an original context, and perhaps can even assign the piece to a particular province or region. In the best of circumstances, with furniture that has had known ownership since it was first made, or better yet was marked by its maker, even specific attribution can be made.

Since in this booklet it has been possible merely to introduce the subject, the list of references on the inside back cover was included for those who would like to delve deeper into Canadian Georgian furniture, one of the finest early decorative arts forms produced in Canada.

# The Furniture

**Armchair, Quebec, Eastern Townships,
c. 1790–1810**
The simple square-legged Chippendale chair
was a widespread English-derivative Georgian
form found from the Maritimes to Ontario;
country versions were made as late as 1825.
Such chairs were constructed of native woods
— maple, birch, cherry, and butternut— but
not of imported mahogany. This example, of
mixed birch and butternut, has an eared back-
rail, a pierced central splat, and bead moulding
around the legs and seat frame, a common
characteristic of this type of chair. (*Canadiana
Department, Royal Ontario Museum*)

**Side chairs, Nova Scotia, c. 1800–1810**
Pierced-slat or "ribbon-back" Chippendale chairs, though popular in England, were uncommon in Canada; they have been found only from Nova Scotia. Such chairs generally had separate slip seats, but these saddle-seated examples, of mahogany and ash, were originally upholstered. They are from an original set of eight made for the Reverend Thomas Trotter of Antigonish, Nova Scotia, shortly after 1800. (*Canadiana Department, Royal Ontario Museum*)

**Corner chair, Nova Scotia, possibly Amherst, c. 1785–1800**
English-Canadian corner chairs are very rare, for they were too specialized for small and non-formal houses. The few known, English in form but of native woods, are from Nova Scotia and New Brunswick. This piece, of dark-stained birch, has an unusual cabriole front leg; the cross-stretchers are clinched in the centre by a large hand-forged nail. (*Canadiana Department, Royal Ontario Museum*)

**Side chair, New Brunswick, c. 1810**
Stylistically mixed furniture, combining Chippendale, Sheraton, Hepplewhite, and Regency elements, was very common in early 19th-century Canada. This mahogany chair, with a Sheraton back and reeded back-rods, has a late Chippendale square-legged, H-stretchered frame. In Canada, chairs of this type seem to have been unique to New Brunswick. (*Canadiana Department, Royal Ontario Museum*)

**Windsor armchair, Halifax, Nova Scotia, c. 1780–90**
**Marked by Joseph DeGant**
Most early Canadian Windsor chairs were of the American type, with rods all around the back, showing the Loyalist influence. Some were maker-marked with stampings on the undersides of the seats. The DeGant chair factory, which opened in Halifax in 1780, was the earliest of many such factories and some of its bamboo-turned chairs, such as this example, were marked DEGANT/ WAR[ranted]. HAL[ifax]. (*Canadiana Department, Royal Ontario Museum*)

**Sofa, Quebec, Montreal area, c. 1790–1810**
Upholstered furniture was uncommon in Canada in the Georgian period, and upholstered sofas and chairs appear to have been limited to households of some wealth. This sofa, with a cherry eight-legged base and a pine upholstery frame, is a late Chippendale style with an obvious Loyalist influence. Framed sofas of this type are known in Canada only from the Montreal area. (*Canadiana Department, Royal Ontario Museum*)

**Sofa, probably Nova Scotia, c. 1805–20**
Later and somewhat more prevalent than Chippendale framed sofas were the
Sheraton-type sofas with exposed arms joined to the seat frame. Most such sofas
now known are from Nova Scotia, but a few have been found in Ontario. This
very fine mahogany piece, with reeded arm posts, has curly maple panels inset in
the upper legs. Maple inlays were quite typically used in combination with
mahogany. (*Ross Memorial Collection. St. Andrews, New Brunswick*)

**Sofa table, Ontario, Napanee area, c. 1810–20**
The sofa table, with short drop-leaves at the ends, was the 18th-century coffee table, but made to stand behind rather than in front of a sofa. A specialized furniture type, it was never common in Canada. This table, of cherry with drawer fronts of bird's-eye maple, is stylistically a New York form, though it was found near Napanee and is quite consistent with the best of Ontario cabinet-making in the early 19th century. (*Canadiana Department, Royal Ontario Museum*)

**Secretary desk, Quebec City, Quebec, c. 1790–1800**
Truly opulent Canadian furniture, which was always specially commissioned, is rare. This secretary, with a bookcase unit above the desk, is of mahogany with secondary pine and poplar. The piece was made in Quebec City, by an unknown English immigrant cabinetmaker, for the Duke of Kent and Strathern (Queen Victoria's father) during one of his periods of service there, either in 1791–93 or in 1796–98. (*Canadiana Department, Royal Ontario Museum*)

**Secretary desk, Quebec, probably Montreal, dated 1805**
**Signed by Jacob Gober**
Canadian low secretary desks typically had hinged doors closing the upper section. This desk is of mahogany and secondary pine; the skirt and sides are surrounded with maple and mahogany band inlays. The classical-column inlays in the upper section are probably English, since motif inlays, like hardware, were generally imported. The right upper door is signed on the back in chalk "Jacob Gober, 1805", though Gober was not necessarily the maker. (*Canadiana Department, Royal Ontario Museum*)

**Bureau desk, New Brunswick, c. 1800–1810**
A more typical Canadian desk type was the bureau desk or *escritoire*, an English
form, in which the writing surface was hinged to make a drawer front and the
entire desk unit slid in and out like a drawer. This example, of mahogany and
secondary pine, is decorated with string inlays in maple, a very common
Maritimes treatment and wood combination. (*Canadiana Department, Royal
Ontario Museum*)

**Drum table, Halifax, Nova Scotia, c. 1810–11**
**Labelled by Tulles, Pallister & McDonald**
Drum tables patterned after the English form, with four drawers and four false drawers, are quite rare in a Canadian context. This table, with a Regency tripod base and reeded legs and pedestal, is of mahogany and secondary pine. It is labelled in two of the drawers. The partnership of Tulles, Pallister & McDonald operated only in 1810–11, and this table is one of only two known pieces by them. (*Location unknown*)

**Drop-leaf table, Saint John, New Brunswick, c. 1820–30**
**Labelled by Thomas Nisbet**
Thomas Nisbet of Saint John, New Brunswick, is the best known of the few early cabinetmakers who labelled their work; some fifty surviving labelled Nisbet pieces are known. This table, with its rope-twist and carved legs and reeded top edges, is wholly of mahogany. The Nisbet label is in the drawer. (*Canadiana Department, Royal Ontario Museum*)

23

**Card or games table, Montreal, Quebec, c. 1810**
Constructed with an extra swing leg to support the hinged leaf, this table is of mahogany and pine, with maple string inlays. It was made in Montreal for Sir James Monk, Chief Justice of the Court of King's Bench from 1794 to 1824. When not open and in use, such tables were usually placed against a wall as side tables. (*Canadiana Department, Royal Ontario Museum*)

**Bracket clock, Montreal, Quebec, c. 1785–1800**
**Marked by François Doumoulin**
Canadian bracket clocks are quite rare, less common even than fine tall clocks. This example, with English works, is mahogany veneered with secondary pine. It is an English form, though by a Quebec-French maker. The brass face of the clock is engraved "Fra.[nçois] Doumoulin/à/Montréal". (*Canadiana Department, Royal Ontario Museum*)

**Tall clock, Quebec, c. 1785–1800**
**Marked by James Orkney**
James Orkney, one of the better-known early clockmakers, worked successively at three locations in Quebec from about 1780 to after 1820. He may have been a Loyalist immigrant, since this clock, with open fretwork above an arched hood, and three brass finials, is a New England type. Made of mahogany, with imported fan inlays in the case and base, the clock has fluted brass-stopped quarter-columns and bracketed base and feet. The brass clock face is engraved "James Orkney/QUEBEC". (*Canadiana Department, Royal Ontario Museum*)

**Dining table, Saint John, New Brunswick, c. 1820–30**
**Attributed to Thomas Nisbet**
Long drop-leaf dining tables, with separate attachable banquet ends, were made by several known Maritimes cabinetmakers, and a number of them by Thomas Nisbet, both labelled and unlabelled, are known. As is most of Nisbet's work, this table is of mahogany, with secondary pine in the under-structure. (*Kings Landing Historical Settlement*)

**Drop-leaf table, Ontario, Niagara Peninsula, c. 1820–35**
Because of the province's later and more scattered settlement, fine Georgian-
period furniture from Ontario is less common than that from the Maritimes and
Quebec. Lacking access to imported mahogany, Ontario makers depended on
native woods, typically cherry and maple, which were used in this table. The
curly-maple end panels are inlaid with cherry, and the light rope-carved legs
have the ball feet that became common on small drop-leaf tables in the 1820s
and 1830s. (*Private Collection*)

**Sideboard, Montreal, Quebec, c. 1800–1820**
Canadian sideboards, which were special pieces, are uncommon, but those that are known tend to be quite elaborate. This mahogany and secondary pine piece, with light reeded legs, has an inlaid oval of satinwood in a rectangle of maple in the upper drawer front. The top and lower case-edges are surrounded with geometric band inlays, as are the upper inlaid rectangle and the cupboard doors. (*Canadiana Department, Royal Ontario Museum*)

**Chest of drawers, Ontario, Niagara Peninsula, c. 1800–1810**
An example of the English rather than the Pennsylvania-German influence in
the Niagara area, this flared-foot chest has sides and drawer spacers of cherry;
the remainder of the piece is of curly maple, some veneered over pine. The
beaded drawer-edge strips and the keyhole inlays are of walnut, another
commonly used Ontario cabinet wood which was often combined with maple
and with cherry. In the early years in Ontario the crafting of sophisticated
furniture was limited largely to the Niagara Peninsula and the Lake Ontario
shoreline. (*Canadiana Department, Royal Ontario Museum*)

**Bow-front chest of drawers, New Brunswick, c. 1805–20**
Maritimes chests of drawers, even the finest ones, often have plain turned feet which seem incongruous to the overall design, though they are original. This piece is wholly of mahogany, with drawer fronts of mahogany veneer over pine. The fluted Sheraton-derived flat side pilasters are an unusual treatment, not typical on chests of this type. Most bow-front chests have only a very slight curve. (*New Brunswick Museum*)

**Candle-stand, Quebec, Eastern Townships, c. 1790–1810**
The candle-stand is a very common furniture form, since candles were the only available means of household lighting until the 1840s. This light and delicate candle-stand is of curly maple; it has an unusual octagonal top and rim strips of pine. The footed cabriole legs are a very typical Georgian leg form for candle-stands and pedestal tables. (*Canadiana Department, Royal Ontario Museum*)

**Combination sewing and writing table, Saint John, New Brunswick, c. 1820 Attributed to Thomas Nisbet**

Specialized sewing tables with suspended work bags are uncommon, and this combination writing-desk form seems to have been unique to Thomas Nisbet of Saint John. The table is of mahogany and mahogany veneers, with fine reeded legs and geometric band inlays. Although unlabelled, it is undoubtedly Nisbet's work and is one of four such pieces by him known at present. (*Private Collection*)